‹ CAMBODIA ›

MAJOR WORLD NATIONS
CAMBODIA

Claudia Canesso

CHELSEA HOUSE PUBLISHERS
Philadelphia

Chelsea House Publishers

Contributing Author: Margie Buckmaster

Copyright © 1999 by Chelsea House Publishers,
a subsidiary of Haights Cross Communications.
All rights reserved.
Printed and bound in Malaysia.

3   5   7   9   8   6   4

Library of Congress Cataloging-in-Publication Data

Canesso, Claudia.
Cambodia / Claudia Canesso.
p.   cm. — (Major world nations)
Originally published: New York: Chelsea House, c1989.
Includes index.
Summary: An overview of the history, geography, economy,
government, people, and culture of Cambodia.
ISBN 0–7910–4732–6
1. Cambodia—Juvenile literature.   [1. Cambodia.]
I. Title.   II. Series.
DS554.3.C35   1997
959.6—dc21   97–23524
CIP
AC

◄ C O N T E N T S ►

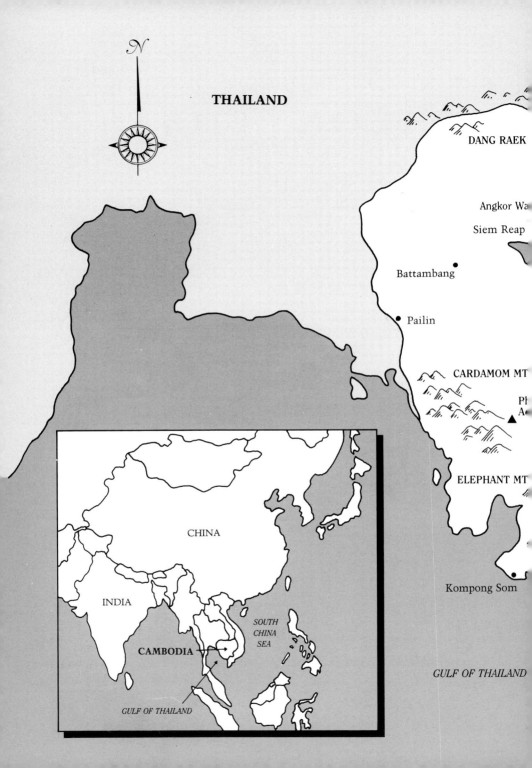

Land Use	Forests, 76 percent; farming, 17 percent; pastures, 3 percent; other, 4 percent
Employment Statistics	Agriculture, 80 percent; public administration and defense, 16 percent; construction, 4 percent
Agricultural Products	Rice, rubber, corn, sweet potatoes, mangoes, beans, oranges, bananas, pineapples
Chief Imports	Food, textiles, medicine and chemicals, minerals and metal products, petroleum
Chief Exports	Rubber, beans, sesame seeds, wood, pepper
Currency	Riel, divided into 100 sen

◄HISTORY AT A GLANCE►

by 350 B.C.	Waves of migrating peoples from the south (Indonesia and Malaysia) and from the north (China and Tibet) meet in Indochina and form new peoples and cultures.
1st century A.D.	The kingdom of Funan is founded in the area that is now Cambodia. Its religion, its language, and much of its culture are borrowed from neighboring India, but its people are Khmers (one of the principal peoples of Indochina).
100 to 550	Funan thrives as a prosperous center of trade between India and China. It dominates Chenla (present-day Thailand) and Champa (present-day southern Vietnam).
late 6th century	The Khmer state of Chenla becomes strong and absorbs Funan.
7th century	Khmer power throughout Indochina first increases, then decreases as Chenla breaks up into many small states.
8th century	Khmer princes from the island of Java establish a strong new state called Kambuja in present-day Cambodia. Culture and religion continue to be influenced by India. Kambuja dominates Indochina for centuries. At its greatest extent, around 1200, the Khmer Empire includes much of present-day Thailand, as well as parts of Laos, Vietnam, and Malaysia.
late 9th century	King Yasovarman I establishes his court and capital in the Angkor region, which becomes the center of Khmer government, scholarship, and worship.

about 1130	The first great temple of Angkor Wat is completed by King Suryavarman II, who also conquers Champa (southern Vietnam).
1177	Rebellious Chams sack the temples and palaces of Angkor.
1181 to 1215	King Jayavarman VII drives the Chams out of Kambuja, builds a huge new capital in the Angkor area, and brings the Khmer Empire to its greatest size and power.
13th and 14th centuries	The Khmer Empire declines. The Annamese people of northern Vietnam conquer Champa. The state of Lan Xang in northern Laos seizes some Khmer territory. An independent kingdom is founded in Siam (present-day Thailand), and the Siamese gradually seize Khmer territory.
1431	Siam captures Angkor. The Khmer capital is relocated at Phnom Penh.
15th to 18th centuries	Cambodia steadily loses territory and power to the Siamese and Vietnamese. By the middle of the 18th century, the king of Cambodia is a puppet of the rulers of Siam and Vietnam.
1862	France acquires control of Vietnam and makes Cambodia into a French protectorate. Together with Laos and Vietnam, Cambodia forms French Indochina.
1941	Norodom Sihanouk is chosen as king by the French shortly before World War II breaks out and Japanese troops occupy Cambodia.
1945	Japan dissolves the French colonial government. King Sihanouk declares Cambodian independence, but France retains some control of the government after the end of World War II.
1953	Sihanouk demands full independence for Cambodia. The French grant it on November 9.

1950s and 1960s	Cambodia proclaims itself neutral in international conflicts, breaks off relations with the United States, and develops closer relations with the People's Republic of China. Some opponents of Sihanouk's rule form guerrilla resistance groups.
1970	General Lon Nol overthrows Sihanouk and forms a new government called the Khmer Republic. The Khmer Republic is supported by the United States, which is engaged in the Vietnam War. U.S. bombers make strikes against suspected bases of Vietnamese communist guerrillas in Cambodia until 1973.
1975	Communist Khmer Rouge guerrilla forces led by Pol Pot take over the country and rename it Democratic Kampuchea. Under Pol Pot's rule, millions of Cambodians die of starvation, execution, torture, or disease. Thousands more flee to refugee camps.
1979	Vietnam invades Cambodia and overthrows the Democratic Kampuchea government. Heng Samrin, a Cambodian supported by Vietnam, is named head of state. The country is renamed the People's Republic of Kampuchea.
1989	The Vietnamese withdraw from Cambodia. Guerrilla warfare spreads through the country, led by three resistance groups: the Khmer Rouge; a noncommunist group called the Khmer People's National Liberation front; and Sihanouk's followers.
1992–93	United Nations efforts result in a peace accord. Sihanouk denounces the Khmer Rouge and again becomes head of state. The Khmer Rouge withdraws from the peace process and resumes fighting. U.N.-supervised elections in 1993 result in the adoption of a new constitution and Sihanouk's formal return to the throne.
1997	Khmer Rouge movement dwindles, but political instability and violence continue as one government faction ousts another.

Princess Norodom Buppha Devi, daughter of Prince Norodom Sihanouk, performs an intricate fan dance. Cambodians have preserved this complex art throughout centuries of foreign domination and internal strife.

Cambodia and the World

One of the 14 nations of Southeast Asia, Cambodia lies at the bottom of the Indochinese Peninsula, a body of land that juts out from the great bulk of China. On the west, the Bay of Bengal separates the peninsula from India. On the east, the South China Sea separates it from the Philippines and the Pacific Ocean. On the south lie the island chains of Malaysia and Indonesia.

This peninsula takes its name of Indochina from its position between the two huge nations of India and China. The five nations that make up Indochina—Burma (or Myanmar), Laos, Thailand, Vietnam, and Cambodia—share many historical and cultural experiences. In recent years, they have suffered from drought, floods, and famines; from conflicts among themselves; and from the widespread destruction brought by the Vietnam War. But although each of the nations has many problems, Cambodia's plight now is perhaps the worst.

Once Cambodia was the heart of a mighty empire of the ancient world, the home of the Khmer people, who ruled much of Indochina from the 9th to the 13th centuries. After a long period of decline, during which the country had little contact with the outside world, Cambodia fell under French control for nearly a century. Following World War II, it gained independence as a modern nation in 1953.

For much of the next 40 years, confusion reigned in Cambodia. The nation had four governments, each of which overthrew the previous government and seized control by force. Larger and more powerful nations, including the People's Republic of China, the United States, the now-disbanded Soviet Union, and Vietnam, vied for control. Decades of civil war, dictatorship, and turmoil destroyed Cambodia's once-thriving farmlands. The destruction brought about dire poverty, hunger, and disease that continue to this day. The country's darkest years were the period from 1975 to 1979, when it was ruled by a dictator named Pol Pot. His systematic destruction of millions of Cambodians has been compared to the horrors of Adolf Hitler's Third Reich.

At times, even the country's name was in doubt. For centuries, it was called Cambodia, a version of "Kambuja," the name of the old Khmer kingdom. After it won independence from France in 1953, it became known as the Kingdom of Cambodia. Then a new government took control in 1970 and renamed the country the Khmer Republic. When Pol Pot seized power in 1975, he outlawed the name Cambodia because it had been used when the country was controlled by the French. He renamed the country Democratic Kampuchea (DK), originating from another version of "Kambuja." Four years later, Vietnam invaded Cambodia, routed the armies of Democratic Kampuchea, and set up a new government called the People's Republic of Kampuchea (PRK), which was supported by Vietnamese troops.

By that time, no one group effectively governed the entire country. Besides the remaining DK forces, at least two other guerrilla organizations fought against the PRK in various parts of the country. Because of Cambodia's fractured government, other nations of the world adopted various attitudes toward the country. Vietnam and the former Soviet Union recognized the PRK as Cambodia's official government. Other nations, including China, believed that the Vietnamese invasion of Cambodia was illegal and felt that the DK was the true government of Cambodia, even though it had lost most of its power. The United States did not recognize either the DK or the PRK.

In 1989, when Vietnam fulfilled a promise to pull out of Cambodia, a peace process finally began in earnest. Under U.N. sponsorship, elections for a National Assembly were held in 1993, and a new constitution was adopted, establishing a democratic form of government within the mold of a constitutional monarchy. Many observers hoped the country might be on the road to a stable peace at last. But by 1997, when the tenuous coalition of parties broke down in a sudden coup, the country seemed to be heading into another round of political confusion and violence.

Phnom Penh's harbor lies on the Mekong River. One of the longest rivers in Asia, the Mekong rises in China and is an important regional waterway.

The Land

Cambodia is a tropical land of densely forested hills, small scattered villages of thatched-roof houses, and emerald-green rice paddies (walled fields that can be filled with water for growing rice). It is bordered by Thailand on the west and northwest, Laos on the north and northeast, and Vietnam on the east and southeast. On the southwest is Cambodia's only outlet to the sea, a short stretch of coastline on the Gulf of Thailand.

The country is about 280 miles (450 kilometers) from north to south at its greatest extent, and about 360 miles (580 kilometers) from east to west. Its total area—including a number of small offshore islands—is 69,898 square miles (181,035 square kilometers), making it about the size of the state of Washington in the United States.

The center of the country is the flattest, most fertile, and most heavily populated and cultivated region. It consists of a moist lowland plain that lies between Cambodia's two major bodies of water: the Tonle Sap (Great Lake) and the Mekong River.

The Tonle Sap is a long, narrow lake in the west central part of the country. During the dry season (November to April), it covers an area of 1,200 square miles (3,120 square kilometers) and is nowhere deeper than 7 feet (2 meters). But during the rainy season (May to October), when it is fed by the waters of many rivers and streams, the Tonle Sap swells to about three times its normal area and reaches a depth of 35 feet (10.5

meters). This annual shallow flooding covers the surrounding countryside with a layer of moist, nutrient-rich mud, ideal for growing rice.

In addition to being the center of Cambodia's rice-growing provinces, the Tonle Sap also provides the country's second main food item: fish. Its warm, shallow waters teem with carp, lake chub, eels, and other species. In fact, the Tonle Sap is one of the richest freshwater fish hatcheries in the world, yielding as much as 26 tons of fish for each square mile. Dried or salted fish is a staple of the Cambodian diet, along with rice. Because of its richness in these two foods, the central plain around the Tonle Sap has been populated since ancient times. Angkor, the old capital and religious center of the Khmer Empire, is located near the northern end of the Tonle Sap.

The Mekong River is one of the longest rivers in Asia. It flows out of the Himalayan Mountains of Tibet (now part of China) and then winds through Laos, along the Laotian-Thai border, and into Cambodia. Within Cambodia, the river runs for approximately 315 miles (494 kilometers)

Rice paddies cover the fertile central region of Cambodia. For hundreds of years rice has been cultivated in these flooded fields, and the crop is a staple of the Cambodian diet.

from the northern border with Laos to the southern border with Vietnam. It then crosses southern Vietnam before emptying into the South China Sea. Fed by the melting snows of the Himalayan peaks and by the torrential downpours of the tropical rainy season, the Mekong reaches its deepest and fastest flow during August and September.

The Mekong is connected to the Tonle Sap by a short channel-like river called the Tonle Sab. This channel joins the Mekong about 65 miles (104 kilometers) south of the lake, where the river sweeps from westward to southward in a huge curve. Just below the junction with the Tonle Sab, a smaller river called the Bassac branches off from the Mekong and flows southward into Vietnam. The curve of the Mekong, together with the Tonle Sab flowing in and the Bassac flowing out, forms a watery X in south-central Cambodia, on the southern edge of the fertile, crowded central lowland. This crossing of rivers is the center of Phnom Penh, Cambodia's capital since the 15th century and its only sizable city.

The Hill of Lady Penh

During the heyday of the Khmer Empire, when the political and religious life of the country was centered at Angkor, the site of present-day Phnom Penh was occupied by a small village. According to Cambodian legend, a lady named Penh lived in that village in a house on a hill. One day the floodwaters of the Mekong washed a huge tree into her house. Inside its hollow trunk she found four bronze statues of the Buddha, the Indian founder of the religion Buddhism, which had become popular in Cambodia. The lady Penh built a temple, or *wat*, on her hill to house the statues.

The temple became famous and was visited by throngs of pilgrims. The people of Cambodia believed that the statues were a sign that the gods wanted a new home. So when enemies from Siam (present-day Thailand) invaded Angkor a hundred years later, the capital was moved to a new site near the temple. The new capital was called Phnom Penh. Phnom means "hill" in the Khmer language, so the city's name means "the hill of the lady Penh." At its center stands a many-towered hilltop temple six centuries old. It is called the Wat Phnom ("hill temple"), and Cambodians believe that it is the one built by the lady Penh for the miraculous Buddhas.

Phnom Penh gradually grew into an important center of commerce on the Mekong River. Junks, barges, and sampans (small, flat-bottomed boats) loaded with traders and their goods plied the river's waters from the city of Luang Prabang in Laos to the Mekong Delta in Vietnam. The shops of Phnom Penh and the huge open-air market called Tuol Tumpoung were among the liveliest spots in Asia.

As Phnom Penh's population and importance grew, the city began to spread out over the surrounding countryside. Many palaces and temples were built. French administrators, who governed Cambodia in the 19th century and the first half of the 20th century, erected government buildings, theaters, and an opera house in the European style. These square stone structures shared the skyline with traditional Khmer architecture, which features buildings that have roofs ornamented with yellow carved serpents and soaring pagodas (towers with many levels). The French also built wide, tree-lined boulevards, broad plazas, hotels, a railroad station, and miles of docks along the muddy riverbanks.

Modern boulevards and traditional architecture made Phnom Penh a fascinating, attractive city before two decades of war devastated this once-thriving capital.

By the time Cambodia gained its independence in 1953, its capital was a thriving, cosmopolitan city that attracted tourists and visitors from all over the world. Its streets were filled with the automobiles of government employees and rich merchants, the *kong dup* (bicycles with a passenger seat attached) that serve as taxis throughout much of Asia, and crowds of pedestrians and vendors. Many people could be seen carrying buckets of water on poles balanced across their shoulders or leading ox-drawn carts whose wooden wheels screeched beneath the weight of heaping loads of farm produce.

The years of civil disorder and warfare that began in the late 1960s took a heavy toll on Phnom Penh, however. First, its population swelled as people from the countryside swarmed to the city to escape bombing and fighting. Slums sprang up, the supply of clean water grew scarce, and the successive governments spent less and less money on the city.

The worst blow fell in 1975, when Khmer Rouge ("red Khmer," or communist) guerrillas under the leadership of Pol Pot overthrew the Khmer Republic and established Democratic Kampuchea. They ordered all cities evacuated because they wanted everyone in the nation to work on the farms. People who lived in the cities were marched out at gunpoint, carrying handfuls of their possessions. Overnight, Phnom Penh became a ghost town, littered with the corpses of those who had resisted the Khmer Rouge. Until 1979, the city was left almost entirely neglected, except for occasional looting and skirmishes between the DK army and anticommunist resistance groups.

Phnom Penh came back to life after the Vietnamese takeover in 1979. Over 100,000 people returned in that year alone. In later years, the population again grew with the addition of U.N. personnel and businesspeople. Today, nearly 45 percent of the population is under the age of 15, including roving bands of homeless children. Estimates place the current population around 920,000.

To aid the recovery, many of the people of Phnom Penh devote some of their free time to citywide cleanup campaigns that are aimed at removing the evidence of war and neglect. Vandalized temples and overgrown parks have been restored, and bullet holes in the walls of buildings have been plastered over.

Phnom Penh's School of Fine Arts, which had been shut down by the Khmer Rouge, has reopened. There, pupils study traditional Khmer dances and crafts. Some students have learned to use the spent brass artillery shells that litter the city and countryside to make religious items— statues of the Buddha of Peace are popular. Electricity is sometimes available. Restaurants have opened, including a few French-style sidewalk cafes that serve Vietnamese beer and food to the many Vietnamese soldiers and administrators who occupy the city. Commerce is bustling in the street markets and in the vendors' sampans moored along the riverbanks. The city on the hill of lady Penh is being reborn.

Other Regions

The central lowland is surrounded by rolling, grassy plains called savannahs. They are slightly higher and drier than the central lowland and have a scattering of trees. In southern Cambodia, these plains run all the way to the Vietnamese border and the sprawling delta of the Mekong River. But to the north, east, and west, the savannahs give way to hilly or mountainous regions covered with dense tropical forest. These are the remote, thinly populated outer districts of Cambodia.

In the north and northwest, the Dang Raek Mountains run along the border with Thailand. The mountains take the form of a 200-mile (322-kilometer) escarpment, or cliff, that rises sheer from the Cambodian plain to heights of from 600 to 1,800 feet (180 to 550 meters). This sandstone cliff forms a natural boundary between the two countries. In the past, however, invading armies have climbed it in both directions. Even in recent decades, secret paths over the cliff have been used by smugglers who traded Cambodian gold for luxury items from Thailand to sell in Phnom Penh's black market. The mountain trails have also been used by Khmer refugees fleeing to camps in Thailand.

In the northeast and east, along Cambodia's borders with Laos and central Vietnam, the country east of the Mekong River is a region of high plateaus, short, steep mountain ranges, and thick forests. Kompong Cham, Kracheh, and Stung Treng, all located on the Mekong, are the major cities of eastern Cambodia. Settlement east of the river is limited to a few small towns and a multitude of tiny villages in clearings in the forest. Travelers use twisting footpaths on the mountain slopes or take canoes along the calmer stretches of the many streams. This inhospitable terrain continues into Laos and Vietnam.

In the southwest, two rugged mountain ranges form a highland region that separates the central lowland from Cambodia's short coastline on the Gulf of Thailand. The more northerly range is the Cardamom Mountains (named for a spice grown and used throughout Southeast Asia). This range rises south of Battambang and Pailin, the two major cities of Cambodia's northwest corner, and runs in a gentle curve parallel to the western shore of the Tonle Sap toward Phnom Penh. Cambodia's highest point, a peak named Phnum Aoral, is located in the Cardamom Mountains. It is 5,949 feet (1,813 meters) high. The other range, the Elephant Mountains, runs along the southern part of the coastline, between the seaport of Kompong Som and the capital city.

The highland region formed by these ranges is sparsely inhabited, difficult to travel in, and unmapped in places. It is a barrier that has long kept Cambodia's small coastal lowland isolated from the more prosperous central lowland. Because the Mekong River has traditionally been used as the main travel route from the central part of the country to the outside world, the coastal region never developed into a major center of trade. In the 1960s, though, a road was pushed through the jungles and the Elephant Mountains to connect Phnom Penh with the coast. Cambodians started building the deep-water port of Kompong Som with help from the United States. After the PRK took control of the country, the work on the harbor was carried on with aid from the Soviet Union. Today, the port handles oil tankers and other ships that are too large to navigate the

Mekong River. The population of the coastal region is growing, and the government plans to develop centers of manufacturing and industry near the port.

Climate and Weather

Cambodia is located between the Tropic of Cancer and the Equator, which means that it is in the world's north tropical zone. Like all tropical countries, it is always hot, or at least warm. (Some tropical countries have cold regions at high altitudes, but Cambodia's mountains, although they are rugged, are not high enough to be cold.)

Daytime temperatures in April, the warmest month, average about 95° Fahrenheit (35° Centigrade). In January, the coolest month, daytime temperatures average 82° Fahrenheit (28° Centigrade). Nights are usually noticeably cooler, but even in the mountains in January a really chilly night is very rare. Frost, snow, and ice are unheard of.

Cambodia has what is called a monsoonal climate, meaning that its weather is governed by strong, prevailing winds called monsoons. These winds create two seasons in Cambodia. During the wet season, from May to October, the monsoon winds blow from the southwest and bring torrential downpours of rain almost every day. The country receives between 75 and 80 percent of its yearly rainfall during this 6-month period. Even when it is not actually raining during the wet season, it is still very cloudy and humid.

Frequent monsoons drench Cambodia during the rainy season.

During the dry season, from November to April, milder winds blow from the northeast. Rain is much less common, and sunshine replaces the clouds of the wet season. Cambodia's total yearly rainfall varies from about 200 inches (5,080 millimeters) on the sea-facing slopes of the Cardamom and Elephant ranges to about 55 inches (1,400 millimeters) in the central lowland.

Plant and Animal Life

Cambodia is shaped something like a bowl. The flat center of the bowl is the central lowland, and its rising sides are formed by the narrow ring of savannah around the lowland and the steeper highlands toward the country's borders. Each of these regions has its own characteristic vegetation.

Since the beginning of history, the central lowland has been given over to cropland. Rice is grown in flooded paddy fields, and corn, tobacco, and other crops are grown in dry fields. Marshy areas around the Tonle Sap and other waterways are often covered with reeds and lotuses (blossoming water plants). The nearby savannahs are covered with grass, which can reach heights of 5 feet (1.5 meters) in the better-watered districts. The lowland and the savannahs have many varieties of fruits and flowers, both wild and cultivated.

The eastern and northern forests have a thick undergrowth of bamboo, vines, rattan (a flexible fiber plant from whose stalk furniture can be woven), and palm trees. From this tangled mass of vegetation rise the hardwood giants of the forest: mahogany, teak, greenheart, and other woods prized by furniture makers and boat builders. Soaring as much as 100 feet (30 meters) above the forest floor, these hardwoods would be the basis of a profitable timber industry if they were not so difficult to reach and harvest. Some scattered logging and forestry takes place west of Kracheh. The harvested timber is floated down the Mekong in giant rafts, with the woodsmen and their families living in huts on top of their harvest.

Pine forests cover the highest parts of the Cardamom and Elephant ranges. Lower down, the mountains are covered with thick tropical rain forests like those of the eastern hills. On the seaward slopes, where the monsoons dump their greatest loads of rain, the forest reaches heights of more than 150 feet (45 meters). The coastal region is largely blanketed in evergreen forests and impenetrable jungles of mangrove trees (low, twisted trees that crowd along the tide line).

Animals native to Cambodia include wild oxen, tigers (now an endangered species), black panthers, spotted leopards (also endangered), bears, numerous species of monkey, and wild boar. Dogs are more common than in neighboring Vietnam, where they are a favorite dish. Centuries ago, the Cambodians domesticated the water buffalo, which is used throughout the country to pull plows and carts.

Elephants are found in the outer districts. Unlike the fierce African elephant, the Asian elephant can be domesticated and trained. Years ago, elephants were used throughout Southeast Asia in heavy labor, such as road making and pulling big loads. Today, they have been largely replaced by tractors, but some elephants and their handlers still find work hauling logs from the eastern forests down to the river at Kracheh.

Herding water buffalo is one of the duties of Cambodian farm boys.

The country has many species of birds, including peacock (whose gorgeous, multicolored tail feathers were a profitable export during the years when they were used in French hats), pheasant, and wild duck. The Tonle Sap area is rich in fish-loving water birds such as egrets, pelicans, and cormorants. Cambodia also has plenty of snakes. Three of the world's most deadly poisonous species—the cobra, the king cobra, and the banded krait—are found there. Fortunately for the Cambodians, most of whom go barefoot all the time, all three species are rather rare.

This imposing temple and the ornate carved reliefs that adorn it bear witness to the splendor of the long-forgotten Khmer Empire.

Early History

Our knowledge of Cambodia's very early history is limited. Archaeologists (scientists who find and study traces of former cultures) have uncovered only three prehistoric sites in the country. Further archaeological work has been postponed since the 1960s by civil war and other disturbances. But from the discoveries that have been made, we know that the earliest inhabitants of Cambodia came to Indochina in several great waves of migration over a period of at least a thousand years.

One wave of people came northward from the island chains that are now called Malaysia and Indonesia. They were brown-skinned people whose way of life involved fishing and growing rice. Another great wave came southward from Tibet and China. These yellow-skinned people possessed metal-working skills and the tradition of domesticating animals. By about 350 B.C., these two waves of migrating people had met in Indochina and blended to form a cluster of new peoples and cultures. The Khmer, who lived in present-day northern Cambodia, were one of these peoples.

These early Khmer lived in small settlements along waterways. They fished, farmed, and raised cattle and pigs. They also hunted, using spears and bows and arrows. Some fragments of pottery, along with a few iron spearheads and polished stone knives, have survived from this prehistoric Khmer culture.

In the 1st century A.D., the first great Khmer civilization arose in Cambodia. It was called Funan. Although the Funanese left no written records and no great buildings, we know of them through the writings of Chinese travelers who visited the country. About 245 A.D. a Chinese ambassador named K'ang T'si traveled to Funan. Upon returning to China, he described Funan as a land so hot that the people wore no clothing, and so rich that taxes were paid in gold, jewels, and precious perfumes. According to K'ang T'si's reports, the Funanese king rode on the back of an elephant that was decorated with diamonds and pearls, and the commoners enjoyed contests between fighting pigs.

Although the people of Funan were Khmers, much of the Funanese culture was borrowed from India. Traders and wandering scholars from India had reached Southeast Asia as early as 100 B.C. Along with trading goods, the Indian travelers brought Sanskrit, the language of their country. In Funan, Sanskrit began to be used for religious writings and court ceremonies (the Khmer language continued to be used for everyday business). The Indians also brought the two great religions of their country: Hinduism and Buddhism. Some Khmer were attracted to Buddhism, but Hinduism won so many followers that it became the state religion of Funan. Hindu gods and rituals became part of Khmer culture.

Funan prospered as a center of trade between India and China. Its merchants received goods from as far away as Persia (now called Iran) and even the Roman Empire. Its craftsmen created magnificent jewelry and religious statues of gold and bronze. Funan had enormous military strength, too. By the mid–6th century A.D., it dominated two neighboring states, Chenla in present-day Thailand and Champa in present-day southern Vietnam. The people of Chenla were also Khmers, but the Chams were Malaysian.

Late in the 6th century, Chenla grew strong and threw off Funan's overlordship. Then, in 598, a king named Bhavavarman claimed rulership of both Funan and Chenla. From that time on, Funan ceased to exist as a separate state. It was absorbed into Chenla.

After taking over Funan, Chenla gained in size and power for a few years. But quarrels among members of the ruling family led to the break-up of the state in the 7th century. It was divided into Land Chenla, a farming culture located north of the Tonle Sap, and Water Chenla, a trading culture along the southern Mekong River. The rulers of Java, an island kingdom in what is now Indonesia, acquired some control over Chenla and took members of the Khmer royal family to live in Java.

The Khmer Empire

In the late 8th century, Khmer princes returned from Java to establish a new kingdom in Cambodia. This new state dominated Indochina for many centuries. It was called Kambuja (from which the name Cambodia is taken), and one of its first great rulers was Jayavarman II, who gained the throne about 802.

Traders, scholars, and warriors have traveled the Mekong River for centuries.

Jayavarman's actions set the patterns for Kambujan society for years to come. One of his most important acts was to declare himself a *devaraja*—that is, a king *(raja)* who was also a god *(deva)*. His rule was absolute and he was worshiped by his people as a god. Believing that their labors on behalf of their ruler would win the favor of the gods and ensure the prosperity of their kingdom, the people devoted much of their time to building magnificent temples and court buildings for the glory of their god-king.

Jayavarman declared Kambuja free of all control by Java or any other state, and he moved the capital from the banks of the Mekong River to a site called Mahendraparvata, northeast of the Tonle Sap. The region around the city became the center of Khmer life. It was distant from attack by Java and other seafaring states and had bountiful supplies of fish and of water for irrigated rice growing. At Mahendraparvata, Jayavarman started a tradition of royal temple building that reached its peak several centuries later in nearby Angkor.

King Yasovarman I moved the capital a few miles from Mahendraparvata to Angkor in the late 9th century. The new capital was a center of scholarship, government, and worship. All of these aspects of Khmer culture continued to be influenced by India. Temples and other structures

The Hindu religion, imported from India, won many Khmer followers. Cambodian artists carved this three-headed figure of Brahma, a Hindu god.

built by the Khmers greatly resemble the heavily ornamented, towered architecture of India. Indian influence was also felt in the lands that are now Burma, Laos, and Thailand. Early Vietnam, however, borrowed more heavily from Chinese culture.

Under Yasovarman's successors, Kambuja expanded by conquering parts of Champa, Annam (northern Vietnam), and Siam (Thailand). It became a powerful state called the Khmer Empire. About 1130, King Suryavarman II honored the Hindu god Vishnu with a huge new temple at Angkor. It was the beginning of a great cluster of temples that came to be called Angkor Wat.

In 1177, rebellious Chams from southern Vietnam invaded Angkor and sacked its temples and palaces. Order was restored to the empire under King Jayavarman VII, who ruled from 1181 to 1215. He drove the Chams out of Kambuja, and his army sacked the Cham capital of Vijaya to avenge the looting of Angkor. The king built a glittering new capital city called Angkor Thom near Angkor Wat.

Under the rule of Jayavarman VII, Buddhism was spread through Cambodia by Indian monks and Khmer Buddhist princes. A religion that teaches people to strive for a level of higher moral purity by performing sacred rituals with the ultimate goal of freeing themselves from earthly suffering, Buddhism offered an uplifting spiritual faith to its followers. Although the Hindu religion continued to provide subjects for statues, literature, and celebrations, Buddhism gradually acquired believers, especially among the common people. By the end of the 13th century, it was the dominant religion of Cambodia and has remained so ever since.

Jayavarman VII brought the Khmer Empire to its peak of power. Under him, the Khmers ruled all of present-day Cambodia and Thailand, southern Vietnam, and parts of Laos, Burma, and the Malay Peninsula of Malaysia. After his death in 1215, however, the empire entered a long period of decline. The Annamese people of northern Vietnam pushed southward and conquered Champa. A civilization called Lan Xang in northern Laos seized territory from the Khmers. But the biggest threat

Members of the Khmer royal family, such as this Cambodian princess, engaged in incessant power struggles from the 1400s to the 1800s as the Khmer Empire disintegrated.

was in the west, where a mixture of Thai and Khmer peoples formed some small states that rebelled against Kambujan rule.

The most powerful of the western states was called Sukhothai. It was founded by one of Jayavarman's sons-in-law, who had been married to a Thai princess. In 1238, Sukhothai successfully threw off Khmer rule. From that time on, the Thai states grew ever more powerful and restless. Eventually they formed a single kingdom, called Siam, and began to press against the Khmer borders. Siam captured Angkor in 1431, and the Khmer rulers had to move their capital to Phnom Penh.

Puppet Kingdom

From the 15th to the 18th century, Cambodia's prestige and power declined steadily. One reason for this decline was the growth of militant and power-hungry neighbors in Thailand and Vietnam. Another was the almost constant fighting among members of the Khmer royal family. Even the peasants and lower classes, who were heavily taxed by the nobles, staged occasional rebellions against their rulers.

During the 16th century, the Khmers tried to take back some of the territory they had lost to Siam. In 1564, the Khmers invaded Siam and entered its capital of Ayutthaya—only to find that it had already been occupied by an invading Burmese army, which promptly drove the Khmers home again. By the end of the century, the Siamese regained their strength and trounced both the Burmese and Cambodians. In 1594, the Siamese captured Phnom Penh.

One of the most tragic episodes in Cambodian history occurred after the fall of Phnom Penh. Having heard reports about strange white men who had appeared in ships along the coasts of Southeast Asia, King Satha of Cambodia decided to see if they could help him save his tottering throne. The white men were the Spanish and Portuguese navigators and traders who opened the Far East to European exploration and commerce in the 16th century. Satha sent a message asking the white men to lend him the support of their powerful and mysterious weapons against the Siamese. As a result, a small Spanish expedition, greedy for loot and adventure, sailed from a base in the Philippines in 1596.

By the time the Spanish reached Cambodia, Satha had been deposed. The Spanish killed the new king and his son and took control of the capital. They then looted Phnom Penh and placed one of Satha's sons on the throne. The Cambodian nobles, however, hated and resented the swaggering foreigners. After a period of complicated plotting and counter-plotting, a conspiracy of high-ranking Cambodians massacred the Spanish in their garrison in 1599. Thus ended Cambodia's first encounter with Westerners. Its next contact with European invaders would not come until the middle of the 19th century.

Between 1603 and 1848, Cambodia had at least 22 kings. Some of them held the throne more than once. Life and politics at the court revolved around plots and intrigue, and a succession of weak monarchs

*Once the flourishing
capital of the Khmer
Empire, Angkor Wat was
abandoned in the 15th
century. Cambodia fell
prey to the ambitions
of neighboring Siam
(present-day Thailand)
and Vietnam and
became a puppet
kingdom.*

sought support from neighboring powers. This strategy only weakened
Cambodia further. For example, King Chey Chetta II, who ruled from
1618 to 1628, declared Cambodia's independence from Siam. In order to
back up these bold words, he asked for help from Vietnam and married a
Vietnamese princess. In a short time, Chey Chetta was forced to pay trib-
ute to Vietnam and to allow many Vietnamese to settle in the southern
part of his country. His successors, hoping to rid themselves of Vietnamese
domination, sought assistance from Siam—and were forced to pay for it by
acknowledging Siamese overlordship of the two northern provinces of Battambang and Siem Reap (which includes Angkor).

This seesaw pattern continued for several hundred years. Only the fact that Siam was engaged in a long series of wars with Burma and that Vietnam was periodically troubled by internal rebellions prevented the two stronger nations from devouring all of Cambodia. Nonetheless, by the time King Ang Eng came to the throne in 1779, Cambodia was a puppet kingdom that owed allegiance to both Siam and Vietnam. Ang Eng was crowned in Bangkok, the new capital of Siam, and placed on his throne by the Siamese army.

Fifty years later, King Ang Chan II asked Vietnam to help him suppress the rebellious forces of his two brothers, who were scheming to usurp the throne. Ang Chan died in mysterious circumstances, and the Vietnamese placed a powerless princess on the Cambodian throne and took control of the country. In 1848, King Ang Duong returned from exile in Bangkok. Helped by Siamese troops, he seized the throne and restored Cambodia's uneasy balancing act, offering allegiance to both of his powerful neighbors.

The four centuries of shifting political fortunes that had followed the invasion of Angkor in 1431 came to an end in the mid–19th century. Instead of bowing to Siam and Vietnam, Cambodia acknowledged a new overlord: France. The arrival of the French in Cambodia marked the beginning of Cambodia's emergence into the modern international world.

A father cradles his wounded daughter as his wife looks on in anguish. The family was one of many driven from their village by Khmer Rouge guerrilla attacks in the 1970s.

Modern History

King Ang Duong reigned from 1848 until 1860. Modern Cambodians honor him as the last king to rule without interference by the French. He did suffer, however, from Siamese and Vietnamese intrusions into Cambodian affairs. Hoping to quell these demanding neighbors, he did what King Satha had done in the 16th century: he asked for help from powerful Europeans who had appeared in the region. This time the Europeans were the French, who wanted to acquire colonies in Southeast Asia.

The Spanish had not arrived in Cambodia in time to help King Satha, and the French did not answer Ang Duong's plea in time to help him. Ang Duong died in 1860 and was succeeded by his son, King Norodom. By this time, the French were growing afraid that the Siamese and the British (who now controlled Burma) might become powerful enough to keep France out of Southeast Asia.

During the 1850s, France had been increasing its pressure on Vietnam to allow French troops in Indochina. In 1862, France forced the Vietnamese to sign a treaty that allowed the French military control over southern Vietnam. Because Vietnam claimed some rights over Cambodia, France decided to take formal charge of Cambodia. In return for a promise of French aid against the Siamese, King Norodom signed a treaty that made Cambodia a protectorate of France. This meant that Norodom ruled only with French permission and that France controlled the country's foreign affairs.

French protection turned out to be a disappointment to the Cambodians. First, France honored Siam's claim to the large provinces of Battambang and Siem Reap in the northern part of the country and turned these provinces over to Siam in 1867 (they were returned to Cambodia in 1907 under a treaty between France and Siam). Then, in 1884, the French bullied King Norodom into signing another treaty that made Cambodia into a French colony. By this time, France also controlled Laos and all of Vietnam. Together, the three colonies came be to called French Indochina.

Although the Cambodians staged an uprising against the French that lasted for almost two years in the late 1880s, France gained more and more power over the daily life of Cambodia. In 1897, France's representative in Phnom Penh took control of the king's Council of Ministers. Norodom's royal power was reduced to insignificant ceremonial functions. He died in 1904, filled with bitterness about the French seizure of his country.

The French built roads and railways in Cambodia, but their main goal was to encourage profitable crops of rice and other products for export. The new roads and railways, therefore, carried Cambodia's produce to ports and markets in Vietnam. Throughout the late 19th century and the early years of the 20th century, Cambodia and the rest of French Indochina remained a quiet, undeveloped colonial backwater.

But as the 20th century progressed, Asia and Africa were swept by waves of nationalism (the belief that each people and nation should be independent and free to govern itself). Colonialism, including France's domination of French Indochina, began to be criticized around the world. In response to this criticism, France built schools and hospitals and claimed to be improving the lives of the Cambodian people. Nevertheless, many Cambodians wished to be rid of the French. One independent-minded Cambodian was Prince Monireth, who was supposed to become king when his father died in 1941. But the French felt that he would be too difficult to control, so they selected another prince, Norodom Siha-nouk, to be crowned instead.

To the dismay of the French, King Sihanouk was dedicated to Cam-bodian independence. When Japanese troops established control over Southeast Asia during World War II, Japan urged Sihanouk to break the treaty with France and declare his country independent. The king took this step in 1945, and a new anti-French government was formed quickly. But just a few months later, after Japan was defeated, victorious Allied forces disbanded the new government and restored Cambodia to France. Some Cambodians who had been part of the anticolonial movement formed an underground resistance group and continued to push for independence.

Independence and Neutrality

For a time, it appeared that King Sihanouk was resigned to having Cam-bodia remain in French hands. When anti-French protesters threatened to undermine his seat on the throne, however, he renewed his demand that France give up its hold on the country. In early 1953, Sihanouk dramati-cally left Cambodia, claiming that he would not return from "exile" until his country was free. The worldwide publicity he received embarrassed France, which had already begun to withdraw from Indochina. The French now speeded up their departure, and Cambodia was declared independent on November 9, 1953. Final withdrawal of French troops from Cambodia, however, was not completed until the end of 1954.

By the mid-1950s, the people of Cambodia—including members of the royal family—had been exposed to the political ideas that formed the basis of modern democratic nations, and they did not want to return to absolute monarchy. They wanted a parliamentary government like that of Great Britain, with both a monarch and a legislature that represented the people.

A new constitution was written, calling for legislators to be elected by the people and for a prime minister to serve as head of the government.

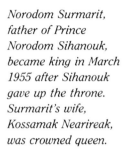

Norodom Surmarit, father of Prince Norodom Sihanouk, became king in March 1955 after Sihanouk gave up the throne. Surmarit's wife, Kossamak Nearireak, was crowned queen.

The king would serve as the formal head of state but would have little to do with the actual government. In order to take an active part in this new system, King Sihanouk gave up the throne to his father (he kept the title Prince) and formed his own political party. He then became the new nation's prime minister, foreign minister, and representative to the United Nations. When his father died in 1960, he also proclaimed himself official head of state.

During the 1950s and 1960s, Sihanouk steered Cambodia on a course of neutrality and stated that he wanted to keep his country free of entanglements with other nations. In spite of this attempt to follow a policy of neutrality, however, Cambodia drifted into a friendly relationship with the communist government of the People's Republic of China. This displeased Cambodia's noncommunist neighbors, South Vietnam and Thailand (formerly Siam). It also angered the United States, which was being drawn into a conflict between the communist government of North Vietnam and the pro-Western government of South Vietnam. Relations between Cambodia and the United States grew so bad that they were completely broken off in 1963. American diplomats were ordered out of Cambodia, and U.S. financial aid programs were stopped.

The 1960s brought growing resistance to Sihanouk's self-centered rule. On one side of the resistance were young communists, many of whom had been educated in Paris. They formed the Communist party of Kampuchea (CPK) and led guerrilla bands throughout the countryside. Sihanouk labeled these rebels the Khmer Rouge ("red Khmer"). The other side of the resistance was made up of Cambodians who favored stronger ties with the United States and other Western nations. This group was headed by General Lon Nol.

By the late 1960s, Sihanouk's hold over his country was being threatened. Lon Nol was elected prime minister, and his government began to disregard the prince's orders. At the same time, the Khmer Rouge grew more active in the remote provinces. Sihanouk was caught in the middle between the two groups. In 1970, Lon Nol's supporters took full control of the government and abolished the monarchy. Sihanouk decided to side with the Khmer Rouge against Lon Nol, even though he did not agree with their communist ideas. He fled to Beijing, China, and tried to influence world opinion against Lon Nol.

After coming to power, Lon Nol had declared a new government called the Khmer Republic. He was supported by the United States, which wanted his help against Vietnamese communist guerrillas who were

No longer king, Prince Sihanouk became prime minister. Upon the death of his father, he centralized power by becoming the head of state.

Backed by the United States, Lon Nol led the Khmer Republic from 1970 to 1975, while the United States hammered Cambodia's countryside with bombs in an effort to wipe out Viet Cong hiding there.

launching raids against South Vietnamese positions from strongholds in Cambodia. U.S. forces and aid arrived in Phnom Penh, but much of the countryside fell under the control of the Khmer Rouge, who fought the U.S. troops side by side with the Viet Cong, or Vietnamese communist guerrillas. As the Vietnam War raged through Southeast Asia, the United States repeatedly bombed places in Cambodia where the Viet Cong were believed to have bases. By 1973, the United States had bombarded Cambodia with three times as many tons of explosives as fell on Japan in World War II.

The Khmer Republic was plagued with problems. Lon Nol and other top leaders fought for power among themselves. Confidence in the government among the common people fell as taxes rose, men and boys were drafted into combat forces, and war and disorder disrupted daily life. The government's dependence on U.S. aid troubled many Cambodians. They wondered how long the support would continue once the war in Vietnam had ended.

At the same time, the Khmer Rouge increased its military strength and began to make inroads into areas formerly controlled by government troops. By 1973, the guerrillas dominated about 60 percent of Cambodia's territory. Sihanouk, in Beijing, claimed to be the head of the Khmer Rouge, but its real leaders were a small group of CPK members who led the jungle fighting in Cambodia. Chief among them was a man known as Pol Pot.

"The Sour and Bitter Time"

Little is known about Pol Pot. He is probably one of the most mysterious and secretive leaders in world history. But the enormous and far-reaching effect he had on the lives of millions of Cambodians is only too well known.

His real name is Saloth Sar (he changed his name after he became one of the leaders of the Khmer Rouge). He was born between 1925 and 1928 in Kompong Thom, in central Cambodia. The son of a peasant family, he is believed to have lived for several years as a monk in a Buddhist monastery during childhood. He became a communist in the 1940s, when he studied at a technical school in Phnom Penh. His academic abilities won him a scholarship to study electronics in Paris. However, he spent more time at meetings of revolutionary societies than in his classes, and he lost his scholarship in 1953.

Returning to Phnom Penh, Pol Pot found work as a schoolteacher and continued his revolutionary activities. Like other members of the CPK, he trained as a guerrilla fighter and became a leader of the Khmer Rouge forces. Opposed to the political factions of both Lon Nol and Sihanouk, Pol Pot hoped to defeat both groups and establish a strict communist rule over the country. He was determined to rid Cambodia of all opponents to Khmer Rouge rule, especially those government officials who had cooperated with the United States while its bombers pulverized the Cambodian countryside.

These Khmer Republic fighters defended the city of Kompong Cham against increasingly fierce Khmer Rouge assaults.

These peasants were forced to plant rice while the Khmer Rouge attacked their village; later, city dwellers were marched to the fields and ordered to farm under the threat of execution.

As the Khmer Rouge grew in power, so did Pol Pot. By 1974, U.S. support for Lon Nol's Khmer Republic had dwindled, and the Khmer Rouge was operating as a formal army. Phnom Penh and other cities were choked with several million refugees trying to escape from the rural fighting between Khmer Rouge and Khmer Republic forces. Farming and other economic activities were at a standstill.

On New Year's Day, 1975, the Khmer Rouge launched an all-out offensive. After three months of constant rocket attacks and heavy fighting, Phnom Penh surrendered in April. The Khmer Republic was dissolved. The stage was set for a new era of government, one that Cambodians today remember as *peal chur chat*—"the sour and bitter time."

The nation was renamed Democratic Kampuchea (DK), and Pol Pot swiftly emerged as its leader. Although he took the title of prime minister, he ruled as a dictator. Every Khmer Rouge soldier was sworn to obey his orders, and citizens who disobeyed the new government's orders were usually put to death. Military officers and government officials who had supported the Khmer Republic were immediately massacred. Almost before the dust of battle had settled on Phnom Penh, Pol Pot set about reshaping Cambodia.

Pol Pot planned to turn Cambodia into a completely self-sufficient agricultural nation modeled on the old Khmer Empire, where the peasant farmers toiled in the fields to produce wealth for the all-powerful government. He ordered his troops to march all residents of the cities and towns into the countryside to work on government farms. Cities, schools, factories, and hospitals were abandoned. Those who resisted their marching orders were executed.

Uneducated peasants, who were now called the Old People, composed the bulk of the Khmer Rouge's members and dominated the DK government. Cambodians who were educated, spoke French or English, lived in the cities, or practiced a skill or profession were called New People. A huge number of the New People, including nearly all of the country's doctors and teachers, were killed. The surviving New People learned to pass themselves off as ignorant farmers to avoid execution. Prince Sihanouk, who had returned from Beijing expecting to have a place in the new government, was confined to house arrest by Pol Pot.

Life in Democratic Kampuchea was a nightmare for everyone but the Khmer Rouge. People lived in terror of what they called *angkar*—"the system" or "the organization." Public executions were carried out almost

Torture was ever present in Democratic Kampuchea. Victims included members of ethnic groups, such as this Vietnamese farmer, as well as almost every educated Cambodian.

The killing fields of Kampuchea have yielded grisly harvests.

daily; prisons and torture centers were full; families were torn apart as men and women were confined to separate barracks on the farms; and any disobedience of Khmer Rouge laws was followed by swift and usually fatal punishment. The DK leaders wanted each person's life to be completely regulated by the state. Religion was suppressed; monks were shot and their temples defaced. The government eliminated schools, postal services, and banks and forbade the use of money.

Thousands of Cambodians escaped across the border of Thailand or died in the attempt. Thousands more died of disease and starvation. Vietnamese and other minority groups living in Cambodia were persecuted with special severity. No one knows exactly how many Cambodians died in Khmer Rouge prisons and work gangs and in the killing fields where mass executions were carried out. Estimates for the number of people who perished during Pol Pot's rule range from 1 to 3 million—out of a population of a little more than 7 million.

A great veil of secrecy was dropped over Cambodia, and other nations learned little about what was going on in the country. Gradually, however, tales told by the desperate refugees who made it to Thailand began to reach a horrified outside world. But international condemnation of Pol

Pot's brutal regime failed to change its policies or bring relief to the Cambodian people.

By the mid-1970s, Democratic Kampuchea was engaged in hostilities with Vietnam, which had become a united country under a communist government in 1975. The problem between the two nations resulted partly from the growing conflict between the Soviet Union and the People's Republic of China. Vietnam had close ties with the Soviet Union, whereas the Democratic Kampuchea government was strongly anti-Vietnamese and was backed by China. The two superpowers encouraged the smaller nations to attack one another.

Pol Pot was happy to oblige his Chinese ally, even though Vietnam had a much larger army and the Cambodian economy was in a shambles. In 1975, DK troops began to make raids on villages inside the Vietnamese border. In retaliation, Vietnam began launching raids into Cambodian territory. By mid-1978, the two nations were engaged in heavy fighting. Late in the year, Vietnam announced that a new Cambodian government had been formed in Vietnam. It was headed by Heng Samrin, a former Khmer Rouge commander who had defected to Vietnam. All that remained was to place Samrin in power.

On December 25, Vietnam invaded Democratic Kampuchea. Vietnamese forces captured Phnom Penh on January 7, 1979. The remnants of the Khmer Rouge and DK forces fled toward the Thai border. One of the Khmer Rouge's last acts before leaving the city was to release Prince Sihanouk from arrest.

Sihanouk found little to celebrate upon his release. A puppet government, controlled by Vietnam, was established in Phnom Penh, with Heng Samrin as prime minister. The nation was renamed the People's Republic of Kampuchea (PRK). Sihanouk was invited to leave the country. He returned to Beijing, after making a speech to the United Nations denouncing Vietnam's invasion.

The United Nations refused to recognize the PRK as the official government of Cambodia. Instead, it allowed DK representatives to hold

Cambodia's seat in the U.N. General Assembly. But this confusion on the international front was far less harmful than the turmoil that continued in Cambodia itself.

The PRK and the Resistance

In the years following the Vietnamese invasion, Cambodia became a land divided by its warring factions. Backed by about 140,000 Vietnamese troops, the PRK controlled most of the country, including Phnom Penh and the harbor at Kompong Som. However, forces that opposed the PRK held some mountainous areas in the west and north near the borders of Thailand and Laos.

These opposing forces fell into three groups. The first was made up of nearly 40,000 surviving members of the communist Khmer Rouge and the DK regime, including Pol Pot. The second group, called the Khmer People's National Liberation Front (KPNLF), consisted of about 15,000 noncommunists who had been fighting the Khmer Rouge since 1975. The third resistance group, headed by Prince Sihanouk, was the National United Front for an Independent, Neutral, Peaceful, and Cooperative Cambodia (FUNCINPEC). This noncommunist group's army numbered 7,000. In 1982, the three groups formed a partnership called the Coalition Government of Democratic Kampuchea (CGDK), but old rivalries wore down the effort and the groups slowly resumed fighting one another as well as the PRK.

As a result of its lack of progress in extending the PRK's control—as well as growing anti-Vietnamese sentiment among the population and continued international pressure—Vietnam withdrew nearly all its troops from Cambodia in late 1989. By then, representatives of 18 countries, four Cambodia parties, and the U.N. Secretary General had met in Paris to begin negotiating a comprehensive settlement. Many months of discussions produced a 1991 agreement that gave the United Nations full authority to supervise a cease-fire, resettle the displaced Khmer along the border of Thailand, disarm and demobilize the rebel armies, and prepare

Hun Sen was a top PRK leader for many years. In 1993, though his party lost the national elections, he forced his way into a coalition as "second prime minister." Then in 1997 he overthrew the first prime minister and took sole control.

the country for free elections. The agreement also paved the way for a new Cambodian constitution, which created a multiparty democracy within the framework of a constitutional monarchy.

Over 4 million Cambodians took part in Cambodia's first free elections in 1993, although the Khmer Rouge, whose forces were never really demobilized, barred some people from participating in the 10 to 15 percent of the country it controlled. Observers hoped that the new government would move toward a long-term peace. By 1997, the Khmer Rouge rebellion appeared to be collapsing, and Pol Pot was ousted from the movement's leadership by his own former comrades — seemingly good news. Nevertheless, the U.N.-brokered coalition government proved too fragile to survive, and in July 1997 a former PRK leader, Hun Sen, led a coup against his rivals. Because alliances among the major individuals and parties have shifted so often, the prospects for long-term stability remain dim.

Two of the 216 faces of Buddha carved on the Bayon seem to gaze serenely over the ruins of Angkor Thom.

Splendors of Angkor

In 1860, a Frenchman named Henri Mouhot was exploring about 150 miles (240 kilometers) northwest of Phnom Penh, not far from the lake called Tonle Sap and the town of Siem Reap. He was a naturalist, collecting samples of plants and insects.

When Mouhot made plans to visit an uninhabited region of dense, scrubby jungle and low hills, his Cambodian attendants showed signs of fear and superstition. He entered the jungle anyway—and was astonished to find huge blocks of crumbling stone, almost completely covered with vines and moss. Hacking excitedly at the foliage with his machete, Mouhot was thunderstruck to discover elaborate carvings on the rocks. Then he realized that the mounds that surrounded him were not hills. They were the overgrown buildings of an ancient, abandoned city. Mouhot had discovered Angkor, the seat of power of the long-forgotten Khmer Empire.

Mouhot's attendants, like the other Cambodians who lived in the area, did not know the origin of the lost city. When the naturalist asked them who had made it, they answered, "The gods made it" or "Perhaps it made itself." They believed that gods had once lived in the city but had abandoned it because they no longer wanted to dwell with the Khmer. Today, however, Cambodians know that Angkor was built by their ancestors, who ruled much of Indochina from the 9th to the 13th centuries.

of the Hindu religion. The earliest temples at Angkor honored Hindu gods; the oldest building that has been excavated was built in 921 and dedicated to the god Vishnu. The temple is called the Cardamom Sanctuary, after the cardamom trees that covered it for centuries after Angkor was abandoned.

Two hundred years after the Cardamom Sanctuary was completed, about 1130, King Suryavarman II completed work on the principal temple of Angkor. With walls more than half a mile (.8 kilometer) long on each side and 30 feet (9 meters) thick, the temple was designed to mirror the universe as pictured in the Hindu religion. Its central towers represent Mount Meru, the home of the gods in Hindu mythology. The walls represent mountains believed to circle the rim of the world. Outside the walls, a water-filled moat represented the endless ocean that was supposed to lie outside the mountains. Like the Cardamom Sanctuary, this enormous temple was dedicated to the Hindu god Vishnu. Its walls were decorated with thousands of delicately carved *apsaras* ("heavenly dancers"), beautiful women who greeted pious Hindus in heaven.

No one knows what Suryavarman's great temple was called when it was built. But a few centuries later, it came to be called Angkor Wat. The new name reflects an important change in Khmer culture. A *wat* is a Buddhist monastery or shrine, and *angkor* is the Khmer word for "capital" or "central city." Angkor Wat means "the temple of the capital." By the time of King Jayavarman VII, in the late 12th and early 13th centuries, the Khmer name Angkor had replaced the Sanskrit name Yasodharapura, and Buddhism had replaced Hinduism as the dominant faith of the Khmer people. A giant stone Buddha was placed in the hall of the highest central tower, formerly sacred to Vishnu.

Jayavarman drove out the Chams, the people from southern Vietnam who had invaded the Angkor region. To celebrate his victory, he built a grand new capital complex of palaces close to Angkor Wat. It was called Angkor Thom ("the big capital"), and it was enclosed by thick stone walls eight miles (12.8 kilometers) on a side. A 300-foot-wide (91 meters) moat filled with snapping crocodiles was a symbol of how fiercely Jayavarman intended to guard his new city.

In the center of Angkor Thom rises Jayavarman's largest monument, a tower called the Bayon. It is carved with 216 faces of the Buddha, gazing in every direction as if to protect the city from surprise attack. The Bayon is also decorated with carved panels, or friezes, that give an astonishingly vivid picture of daily life in the Khmer Empire: fishermen casting nets, women in the marketplaces, builders carrying palm-leaf thatch for roofs, and children driving wooden ox-carts. As one Cambodian visitor to Angkor remarked during the 1960s, "Kings have come and gone, but life for the villager has changed little over the centuries."

Angkor was abandoned in the 15th century. Rebellious Siamese princes threw off Khmer rule and sacked the Khmer capital in 1431. After this humiliating defeat, the Khmer court made its capital in Phnom Penh. The Siamese in turn withdrew from Angkor, and the temples and palaces were left to the rain and the jungle for centuries.

The passing time was not kind to the ancient buildings. Foundations shifted, toppling walls and causing ceilings to cave in. Moss and other vegetation gradually covered just about everything, leaching away the surface of the stone with acids created by the plants. Most destructive of all, seeds from the droppings of birds lodged in crevices in the stones and took root. Eventually, the roots and branches of sturdy banyan trees began to tear apart even the mightiest buildings.

The Angkor Conservancy was able to undo much of the damage caused by time and nature during its term as caretaker of the site. The organization removed the corrosive moss, steadied the foundations with concrete, and replaced badly crumbling blocks with exact replicas made from local sandstone. But the protective efforts of the Conservancy came to an end in 1972, when spreading warfare between Khmer Republic and Khmer Rouge forces caused work at Angkor to be abandoned. After that time, the ruins were off limits to the outside world. Between 1975 and 1979, the Khmer Rouge regime refused all requests from scientists to visit

Traditional dances and the towers of Angkor Wat are reminders of the glories of Cambodia's past. Reliefs on the walls of Angkor Wat show that the dances have changed little over many centuries.

Angkor. Refugees from Democratic Kampuchea told stories of vandalism and destruction. Many refugees also carried pieces of the carvings or the stone heads of statues, hoping to sell them to collectors in Thailand. Historians and archaeologists throughout the world wondered whether Angkor would survive the turmoil in Cambodia.

When the Vietnamese-backed PRK took over in 1979, it promised a new program of restoration and preservation for Angkor, with help from India. Tourists were even welcomed for the first time since 1972. Still, guerrilla warfare continued to rage in the surrounding areas. In 1997, fighting erupted again around Angkor, and land mines have been found nearby. Many of the smaller artifacts have been removed to museums for safekeeping.

After its discovery in 1860, Angkor captured the imagination of the world. It became a symbol of Cambodia's exotic beauty and its proud, ancient heritage. During the 1980s, the distinctive three-tiered towers of Angkor Wat appeared on each of the flags flown by the warring factions. The newly unified country's flag now includes horizontal bands of blue, red, and blue with a white representation of Angkor Wat outlined in black at the center of the red band.

Farmers gather for the distribution of rice seeds at Kompong Thom.

People and Cultures

Of Cambodia's estimated population of 10,861,000, about 90 percent are members of the dominant ethnic group, the Khmer. They speak Khmer, the official language of the country, although many of them also speak some French or Vietnamese. The Khmer tend to be short (the average height for men is about 5 feet 3 inches, or 160 centimeters) and muscular, with straight black hair and dark brown or black eyes. About half of all Khmer have the epicanthic fold (the fold of skin over the eyelid that gives a distinctively almond-shaped appearance to the eyes of many Oriental people).

Many Khmer still dress in the traditional clothing that their ancestors adopted centuries ago: a *sampot*, or knee-length, wraparound skirt, topped by a white tunic or blouse. But many Khmer men prefer Western-style outfits of trousers and short-sleeved shirts. In the years when Pol Pot's troops were enforcing a brutal form of social equality, everyone was forced to wear black. Today, people prize bright colors and lively prints for sampots and shirts. One traditional item still worn by all country Khmer and many city dwellers is the *krama*, a checkered cloth that can be wrapped around the head turban-style or worn as a scarf or shawl. Most kramas are white with black checks, but the Khmer Rouge still wear red-checkered headdresses.

Of the minority ethnic groups in Cambodia, the Vietnamese are probably the largest. Most estimates place Cambodia's Vietnamese population at 5 percent of the country's total. The southern part of Cambodia has always had many inhabitants of Vietnamese descent. But although the two nations are close together geographically, they have a long history of mistrust, dating from centuries of conflict over the territory around the Mekong River delta. Before 1975, the Khmer looked down upon the Vietnamese Cambodians, often referring to them with a term that meant "savages from the north." The Vietnamese, in turn, kept themselves separate from the Khmer, living in their own communities in the eastern part of the country.

The situation changed during the 1970s. Beginning with the Lon Nol regime and continuing under Pol Pot, the Vietnamese minority in Cambodia was targeted for persecution. Many Cambodians of Vietnamese descent fled to Thailand or were deported to Vietnam. Many others were killed. On the other hand, when Vietnam installed the PRK government in Phnom Penh, Cambodians of Vietnamese descent gained high status in official circles, and additional Vietnamese came to live in Cambodia with PRK encouragement. After Vietnam's troops withdrew, the tables turned again. In 1993, for example, around 20,000 ethnic Vietnamese had to flee the Tonle Sap region after Khmer Rouge attacks. Today the position of Vietnamese in Cambodia remains uneasy.

Many ethnic Chinese also found themselves targets of persecution during the 1970s and 1980s. Until 1975, most shops and small businesses were owned by the Chinese, who were regarded as the country's most skilled traders and businesspeople. Beginning with the Khmer Rouge takeover, however, the Chinese found their position precarious. Many of them learned to speak Khmer and became farmers, taking care not to call attention to themselves by dressing or talking in a distinctively Chinese fashion. During the Vietnamese occupation they were unpopular with both the official government and the Khmer Rouge opposition. In recent years, they have slowly begun to resume their old role

(continued on p. 73)

Scenes of
CAMBODIA

⋏ *A family in Phnom Penh offers up prayers and gifts of food and beer to the spirits in February 1975, as Khmer Rouge guerrillas fire rockets at the besieged capital city.*

◄ *Schoolgirls arrive at Phnom Penh's stadium for a ceremony in honor of French president Charles de Gaulle in 1966. Bright balloons float above helmeted soldiers and guards in the background.*

➤ *Drawing on all their balance and poise, girls perform a traditional dance called the* lamthon.

ⵎ *Typical tasks of farm girls include gardening and preparing food. This young girl wears the traditional head scarf, the* krama.

➤ *Each morning, Buddhist monks stream out of this Phnom Penh temple to gather donations of food from passersby.*

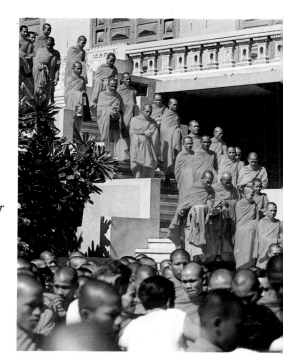

∧

◄ *This small temple (above) at Angkor Wat was built by Jayavarman VII and was dedicated to his parents. The magnificent ruins of Angkor were damaged by centuries of jungle overgrowth, but more recent enemies have included violence and vandalism. The frowning faces of statues (left) bear fresh gouges and chips caused by gunfire.*

▲ *During anti-Communist student riots in Phnom Penh in 1970, a young man holds aloft a picture of Prince Norodom Sihanouk. The prince's rule had been overthrown, and he was living in China.*

➤ *Modern farming equipment, such as this tractor, is rare in Cambodia; most work is done by hand. These women are gathering rice from a paddy field.*

⋏ *An armed soldier stands guard at the water festival.*

∧ Cambodian refugees at a camp in Thailand are herded aboard buses for the return to their homeland after the fall of Democratic Kampuchea.

(continued from p. 64)

in Cambodian society. Today, about 1 percent of the country's people are ethnically Chinese, and they live mostly in Phnom Penh and other large towns.

Another minority group within the population consists of the Khmer Loeu, or hill people. They are members of a number of small, scattered tribes that live in the most remote highland regions of the west, north, and east. They speak their own languages, which cannot be understood by the Khmer of the central lowland. Both men and women among the Khmer Loeu usually wear only short loincloths and several strings of beads.

Traditionally, the hill people were shy and elusive roving hunters, not farmers. In recent years, however, they have adopted many of the customs of the lowland Khmer. Some younger members of the hill tribes now work on farms and mingle easily with other ethnic groups. Before many more years have passed, the Khmer Loeu culture will probably have been absorbed into the mainstream of Cambodian society.

Cambodians crowd the riverbanks and peer from houseboats at the pirogues proceeding slowly upstream during a water festival held in Phnom Penh in 1962. Today, religious festivals have again become acceptable after being banned by Pol Pot.

The remaining ethnic groups in Cambodia consist of a small number of Burmese, most of whom live in the north near the city of Battambang, and a still smaller number of Chams, descendants of the ancient Kingdom of Champa in the south. The Burmese are the descendants of miners and jewelers who came from Burma to work in the ruby mines of Pailin during the French colonial era. The Chams are a Vietnamese-Malaysian people who live in southern rural communities. Their close-knit way of life has been disrupted by Cambodia's turbulent political atmosphere, and they are beginning to be absorbed into the Khmer population.

At one time, Cambodia's population included small numbers of Thais, Laotians, Europeans, and Americans, but these groups fled or were evacuated when the communist regime came to power. Encouraged by the relative peace of the mid-1990s, some members of these groups have returned to Cambodia.

Religion, Daily Life, and Customs

In recent times, the daily life of the Cambodians has been greatly affected by the new ways violently forced on the country by Pol Pot's regime and by the people's attempt to adjust to Vietnamese domination. A bewildering mixture of new rules and social patterns that conflict with the traditions of the past has left the Cambodian people confused and uncertain about what values are acceptable in modern Cambodia. Gradually, however, many of them are returning to their traditional ways of living. One good example of the Cambodians' renewed interest in old customs is the rebirth of religion.

Under Pol Pot, religious activity was forbidden and Buddhist monks were forced to leave their monasteries to work in the fields. Today, the monks have returned to their monasteries, and Buddhist festivals once again punctuate the Cambodian year. In 1994 the supreme patriarch of Theravada Buddhism was nominated for the Nobel Peace Prize because of his efforts for national reconciliation.

About 2 percent of Cambodians are Muslims; this group includes all of the Chams and some Khmer of the south. Many of the Vietnamese are Roman Catholic, and almost all of the Chinese are Taoist (Taoism is a belief system that originated in China centuries ago). The hill people are animists, who believe that magical spirits live in the natural world, such as in trees, rocks, or rivers. Each community of hill people has an *achar*, or spirit doctor, who leads religious ceremonies during which he claims to communicate with the spirits.

By far the most important religion in Cambodia is Buddhism. About 95 percent of Cambodians—nearly all the Khmer—are Buddhists. They believe that certain acts earn merit, making it easier for a good Buddhist to be reborn into a better life. Men earn the greatest amount of merit by entering a monastery. For this reason, many Cambodian boys spend a year or two as junior monks. Even if the novices leave the monastery, they have acquired a great deal of merit. Women earn merit when a son becomes a monk. Other merit-earning deeds include visiting shrines, feeding monks, and celebrating holy days.

Cambodian Buddhism is an easygoing faith and does not forbid belief in spirits and magic. As a result, even the most devout Khmer Buddhists share a little of the hill people's animism. Khmer communities have achars who share in the spiritual guidance of the people but do not compete with the Buddhist monks. Most weddings, funerals, and coming-of-age ceremonies honor both the Buddha and the local spirits. For example, when boys and girls enter their teens, they are blessed by a Buddhist monk. At the same ceremony, the neighborhood achar tells the child's fortune and cuts off his or her hair—to trick the evil spirits who are believed to hide in hair. Nearly every Cambodian home has a small statue of the Buddha in a place of honor, with offerings of flowers or cigarettes in front of it, as well as a tiny spirit house decorated with colored flags to keep the local spirits happy.

Before the disturbances of the 1970s, most of Cambodia's population lived in small rural villages. During the early 1970s, Phnom Penh and

The monsoon floods that make rice paddies in the Tonle Sap area so productive also make it necessary for most houses there to be built on stilts.

other urban centers mushroomed as refugees streamed in from the countryside. When the Khmer Rouge ruled the country, the cities were abandoned and whole segments of the population were forcibly relocated to new parts of the country. Today, most Cambodians live in rural areas, and most people have returned to their former homes.

The typical Cambodian village has about 300 people. They live in small houses strung out along a roadway or waterway. All of the houses are built on wooden stilts to keep them above the mud and floods of the wet monsoon season. The smaller and poorer homes consist of a single room with one door and no windows. They are made of woven palm leaves and poles. Larger and wealthier homes have several rooms that include windows and plank floors and walls. The wealthiest homes have sheet-metal roofs instead of palm-leaf thatch.

Most houses have one or two tall, bristly sugar palms growing nearby. These trees are found everywhere in Cambodia. They provide fruit, a sweet syrup used in cooking, and thatch for roofs. Morning and evening, a child will scamper as much as 50 feet (15 meters) up a rickety homemade ladder of twigs to gather the tree's sweet sap.

Inside the houses, a family's simple assortment of furniture may include bed mats and storage chests, baskets, water jars, and perhaps low tables for eating. Cambodians usually eat in a squatting position, with feet flat and knees sharply bent. Even the smallest Cambodian child can squat quite comfortably in this position for hours.

The staple foods of the country are rice and fish, which may be fresh, dried, or salted. Most families grow enough rice on their small private farms for their own use, and people gain additional earnings by working on large, government-owned farms. Potatoes, onions, chili peppers, bananas, coconuts, eggplants, tomatoes, and mangoes are also cultivated, although a single family can usually manage to grow only two or three different crops. Some of the garden produce will be used at home, and the rest will bring in a little cash at the local market.

The fish come from the Tonle Sap, where the fishing industry has created a unique lifestyle. Fishermen and their families live in small huts on floating rafts or on stilts in the shallow water at the lake's edge. Beneath each hut is a large underwater box made of bamboo or woven reeds. Fish are captured, then kept alive in the box and fattened on corn meal and other foods. When they reach the desired size, they are sold live or dried. These *trung trei*, or fish farms, offer a livelihood to perhaps 40,000 families. Other fishermen from nearby villages harvest the lake's bounty using nets and poles.

The fish farmed and netted in the Tonle Sap feed thousands of Cambodians.

Fruit of all kinds is a treasured food treat in Southeast Asia, but one fruit is especially popular in Cambodia. It is the durian, which is famous for its delicious, sweet-tasting, creamy interior—and also for its horrible, stomach-turning smell. For a few weeks after durians ripen, some markets and eating houses have special walled-off sections where durian lovers can enjoy their exotic treat without discomforting the other customers.

Another product that is sold in every market in Southeast Asia is the betel nut, a mildly narcotic seed that is wrapped in leaves and chewed. Betel nut turns the teeth and gums of users dark red, but darkened teeth are a sign of beauty to Cambodians, who feel that white teeth are unlucky because they look like a skull. Even Cambodians who do not chew betel nut often deliberately darken their teeth with paste. Some wealthy people have their front teeth replaced with gold or even rubies.

Like the Chinese and Vietnamese, Cambodians generally eat with chopsticks. A typical meal consists of a bowl of fried or steamed rice, mixed with bits of fish and seasoned with chilies, mint, or garlic. More elaborate meals include such treats as barbecued shrimp, *pong tea kon* (duck eggs eaten just before the ducks are ready to hatch), Chinese noodles, roasted sunflower seeds, *chong roet* (charcoal-broiled cicadas), and *ansamcheks* (rice cakes with banana centers). Tea is the national drink.

The Arts

Cambodians have had little time for the arts in recent years. The national ballet and theater companies established by Prince Sihanouk were closed down by later governments, and Pol Pot ordered craftsmen to leave their workshops and labor in the fields. But Cambodia has a long history of artistic achievement, and the arts and crafts of its people have been revived despite the political uncertainties.

Music is probably practiced more widely than any other art form. Nearly all Cambodians sing, either making up their own songs as they work or repeating traditional songs. Many also play instruments. Cambo-

Music pervades Cambodian life. Even this young soldier carries her guitar with her.

dian music uses gongs, drums, flutes, wooden xylophones, and *tros,* or one-stringed violins.

The national dance, called the *lamthon,* involves slow, graceful motions of the hands and arms. The most highly trained lamthon dancers wear elaborate, tight-fitting costumes of silk and velvet that must be sewn onto them before each performance, but village girls in their sampots dance the lamthon with equal charm. The delicate poses and gestures that are used in the dance have an ancient heritage, for they resemble those shown on the sculpted figures at Angkor Wat.

Cambodian plays usually include music and dancing. Some are based on very old stories about Hindu gods and heroes. Other plays feature comic tales about beautiful princesses, greedy merchants, bashful lovers, and other characters from folktales. These comic plays are usually performed at weddings and festivals by wandering bands of actors.

Among the crafts traditionally practiced in Cambodia are jewelry making, wood and stone carving, and gold- and silversmithing. Most of the jewelry and craft items made by Cambodian artisans are based on ancient religious designs. Popular craft items include dancers' ankle bracelets decorated with tiny silver bells, sandstone statues of the Buddha, and wooden panels on which are carved scenes from the *Ramayana,* a centuries-old Hindu religious epic. Except that they lack signs of wear, craft objects made in Cambodia today look as though they had come straight from the ruins of a Hindu temple or an early Buddhist shrine.

Rubber is Cambodia's second most important export, but little of it is used in Cambodian manufacturing. Aging machinery, political chaos, and a lack of spare parts and trained workers have limited industrial production.

Government and Economy

For a brief time in the 1990s, Cambodia achieved a degree of government unity. But this period of stability ended in 1997, and some observers feared a new era of confusion and violence. For most of the past few decades, the country has been a patchwork of several different government systems, each controlling a separate area and a different part of the population. For many years, no one government could truly claim to control Cambodia. To understand today's Cambodian government, one has to understand the country's recent political history.

After driving the Khmer Rouge from power in 1979, the PRK regime, supported by large numbers of Vietnamese troops, controlled the largest part of Cambodia during the 1980s. The PRK governed Phnom Penh, most of the central lowland, and the eastern and southern parts of the country. The leaders of this government were Heng Samrin and Hun Sen.

The PRK was organized much like the communist government of Vietnam. Its single political party was called the Kampuchean People's Revolutionary Party (KPRP), and its legislative body was known as the National Assembly. This Assembly included 117 members, representing all regions of Cambodia under PRK control. Because the members of the National Assembly were elected, the PRK claimed that the people of Cambodia had a say in their government. However, all candidates chosen for the election were selected by the PRK's political advisers.

Three anti-PRK forces (the communist Khmer Rouge and two noncommunist organizations) grouped themselves together as the Coalition Government of Democratic Kampuchea (CGDK) and managed to keep control of small areas in the north and west. These resistance forces had many supporters among the 225,000 Cambodians living in refugee camps along both sides of the Thailand-Cambodia border. In addition, the various CGDK forces controlled other areas, notably in the provinces of Battambang and Siem Reap in the west.

Each of these three groups kept its own government that administered the camps or communities within its areas of dominance. They regarded the CGDK not as a permanent government but merely as an aid to overthrowing the PRK. All three groups promised that, if the PRK regime were toppled, the Cambodian people would be free to choose their own government.

When the Vietnamese, bowing to international pressure, withdrew from Cambodia in 1989, they left the PRK government to face a rebel coalition backed by China and Thailand. That same year, under U.N. auspices, all four major Cambodian parties plus representatives of 18 other countries convened in Paris to begin working out a settlement that would guarantee a genuine self-determination and basic human rights for the Cambodian people.

The United Nations established its own transitional authority in Cambodia and undertook a large-scale resettlement of refugees from Thailand. Prince Sihanouk, himself returned from exile, became the head of an interim council. When the first elections were held for a new National Assembly in May 1993, there were a number of political assassinations, and rival parties accused each other of inciting the violence. In addition, the Khmer Rouge boycotted the elections, tried to keep people from voting, and terrorized ethnic Vietnamese. Nevertheless, about 90

Part of Cambodia's recent history is the story of streams of refugees—between rural villages and cities in the 1970s and across the borders to camps in Thailand in the 1980s.

percent of the eligible voters—over 4 million Cambodians—participated in the elections. The FUNCINPEC party, which supported Sihanouk, won the greatest share of the votes and soon established a coalition with the Cambodian People's Party, the heir of the old Vietnamese-backed PRK. The 120-member Assembly then drafted and approved a new constitution that established a constitutional monarchy. Sihanouk, now dubbed "King" rather than "Prince," was formally restored to the throne as head of state. The new Royal Cambodian Government, as it was called, was led by First Prime Minister Prince Norodom Ranariddh of FUNCINPEC (Sihanouk's son) and Second Prime Minister Hun Sen of the Cambodian People's Party.

Many observers believed that the new constitution and government were a major step forward for Cambodia. Nevertheless, serious problems remained. The Khmer Rouge continued their guerrilla warfare until the movement splintered in 1997. Ranariddh's half-brother, Prince Chakrapong, rejected the election results, tried to entice the eastern provinces to secede, and then attempted a coup in 1994. Even within the national government, the coalition of rivals soon collapsed, and in 1997 Hun Sen led a coup that forced Ranariddh to flee the country. In these conditions, the ultimate form of Cambodia's government remains uncertain.

Education and Health

The Khmer people's long tradition of education for boys in Buddhist monasteries was expanded by the French, who built many schools (including some girls' schools) in the first part of the 20th century. But this educational tradition was destroyed by Pol Pot, who felt that education was unnecessary and that citizens should merely listen to and obey the orders of their government. The Khmer Rouge closed the schools and executed the teachers.

Although attempts have been made to rebuild the schools since then, shortages of teachers, books, and funds—not to mention ongoing strife in parts of the land—continue to plague the education system. Estimates of literacy vary widely, but it is probably true that less than 40 percent of all adult Cambodians can read and write. Even if the government remains relatively stable, significant improvements will likely be slow.

Health care has suffered from the effects of war, too. The French built a number of hospitals when they governed Cambodia, yet even then the country did not have enough doctors or medical clinics. The recent decades of war have made the health-care situation even worse. Pol Pot closed most of the hospitals and forced their medical staff to work in the fields. Many doctors fled or were killed. By the time the Khmer Rouge regime fell in 1979, only 60 remained of the 600 doctors who had been working in the country 4 years before. Although the situation has improved, there is still only 1 doctor for every 14,000 Cambodians. It will be a long time before Cambodia's health-care programs approach those even of other underdeveloped nations.

At present, life expectancy is around 50 years for both men and women. The infant mortality rate (the number of babies that die during their first year) is 108 deaths per 1,000 births, compared to a rate of 24 in nearby Malaysia. The major causes of death—aside from war—are tuberculosis, malaria, and pneumonia.

Health care is plagued by shortages — of hospitals, supplies, and personnel. Thousands of medical professionals died in Pol Pot's "restructuring" of Cambodian society.

Economy, Transportation, Communication

Like its educational and health-care systems, Cambodia's economy has been badly damaged by years of war, neglect, bombing, and mismanagement. The economy has always been based on agriculture, but in past years Cambodia was productive and fruitful, managing to feed its people well and to export large amounts of rice and fish.

Agriculture remains the chief economic activity, accounting for 80 percent of the country's total production each year. Rice is the major crop, followed by rubber and a variety of vegetables and fruits. The few industries include fish processing, a little timber harvesting, and the production of small amounts of basic goods, such as cement, shoes, and textiles.

Cambodia imports from other countries many more goods than it exports. Export products include rubber, timber, beans, sesame seeds, and pepper. Imports include food, textiles, medicine, pesticides, plastics, minerals and metal products, electrical and electronic equipment, and petroleum.

During the mid-1990s, the country enjoyed strong growth in construction and services, and inflation dropped from 26 percent in 1994 to only 6 percent in 1995. Imports increased as a result of external financing, and total exports increased because of a rise in log exports. The country also has received substantial international support.

People and goods travel mostly along the inland waterways or by road. The inland waterways—mostly the Mekong and Tonle Sab river systems—have a total length of about 1,200 miles (1,930 kilometers). Roadways total 8,296 miles (13,358 kilometers), of which about 20 percent is paved. The country's main thoroughfare is a four-lane highway between Phnom Penh and the port at Kompong Som. Most of the roads are dirt or gravel tracks, which are often washed out by floods or made impassable by slippery mud during the rainy season.

Most Cambodians will probably never ride in an automobile. The country has fewer than 30,000 passenger cars and about 9,000 commercial vehicles. Most of the vehicles are found in or near Phnom Penh. Country people who have to travel do so on foot or by ox cart. City residents ride bicycles or pedicabs (bicycle-powered taxis).

The railway system has been hard-hit by the decades of fighting, since train lines are a favorite target of attack for guerrilla and bandit groups, especially the Khmer Rouge. In the first six months of 1995, over 300 sections of track were blown up. Even when free from sabotage, the train service is limited. The country has two basic lines built by the French, running south and north from Phnom Penh. The trains are used mostly for freight rather than for passenger service. Estimates place the total length of track at about 380 miles (roughly 600 km).

More than 30 Khmer publications provide news to Cambodians,

Siem Reap, once the scene of this placid market, became the site of some of the heaviest fighting between Vietnamese-backed and anti-Vietnamese forces in the late 1980s.

These Cambodians gather in Phnom Penh to read newspapers and perhaps share gossip, but most of the nation hears the news over the radio.

along with two French-language newspapers and three English journals. There is one state-owned television station and one private station, although many hotels now have satellite dishes that pick up broadcasts worldwide. Some estimates say that only about one in every 130 Cambodians has a television, and telephones are much rarer still. But there is a radio for approximately every 11 people in Cambodia. Radio is therefore a major supplier of news, and the sources of radio broadcasts include Radio France Internationale, the BBC, and Radio Australia.

These Cambodian children on their way to a refugee camp were on their way to an uncertain future as well. Despite the decline of the Khmer Rouge, many areas of the countryside are far from secure.

Cambodia in Review

Today, the confusion that has surrounded nearly everything connected with Cambodia seems to be continuing. Efforts to establish political peace and stability have repeatedly failed.

In recent decades, the country has been controlled by a number of separate, competing governments. Long periods of civil war pitted communists against noncommunist groups. The communist organization called the Khmer Rouge ruled Cambodia from 1975 to 1979, forming a regime called Democratic Kampuchea (DK). The DK was headed by Pol Pot, whose policies of systematic extermination and relocation killed millions. Today, the Pol Pot regime is counted among the cruelest and most nightmarish governments of modern times.

When he was chased from power, a Vietnamese-backed government controlled most of the country for another decade. Finally, in the early 1990s, a coalition government effectively united many factions under a renewed Kingdom of Cambodia, and the breakup of the Khmer Rouge movement in 1997 may finally have nullified the most important guerrilla group. Nevertheless, a new coup in 1997 placed the future in doubt.

Most Cambodians belong to the Khmer ethnic group. Their culture and language reflect a blending of their Hindu, Chinese, Tibetan, and Malaysian ancestors. They are most familiar to the world today as victims of oppression or refugees from their war-ravaged homeland. But for 500 years, from the 9th century to the 14th century, the mighty Khmer Empire ruled most of Indochina. Religion and the arts flourished in this ancient empire, which left behind one of the most impressive architectural monuments ever created—the temples and palaces of Angkor Wat. Discovered in the 1860s and closed to the world a century later by war in Cambodia, Angkor Wat is a priceless piece of the world's historical and artistic heritage. People around the world hope that the present troubles in Cambodia will not destroy the magnificent ruins.

Indochina has long been one of the world's great crossroads. In ancient times, it was the meeting place of such distinctive cultures as those of India, Malaysia and Indonesia, and China. When Europeans began to explore and trade throughout the world, they realized that the location of Southeast Asia made it a perfect site from which to control the commerce and politics of the Far East.

Since the downfall of the Khmer Empire in the 14th century, Cambodia has been at the mercy of more powerful nations. For centuries, the king of Cambodia was a puppet whose strings were pulled by Thailand and Vietnam. Then the French marched into Cambodia and controlled the country for almost a century. Cambodia won independence in 1953 but enjoyed only a short period of peace. Once civil war broke out, the competing groups found backing from the United States, China, and Vietnam—all larger countries with interests of their own. Today, the United States supports efforts in Cambodia to build democratic institutions, promote human rights, foster economic development, eliminate corruption, and improve security—conditions that the long-suffering people of Cambodia richly deserve.

◄ G L O S S A R Y ►

Achar	The spirit doctor, sorcerer, or fortune-teller of a Khmer community.
Angkar	Khmer for "the system" or "the organization." It was used by Cambodians to refer to the Pol Pot government's brutal program for changing Cambodian society.
Angkor	The Khmer word for "capital," which was used to refer to the extensive city complex built by the Khmer rulers.
Democratic Kampuchea (DK)	The communist regime that ruled Cambodia from 1975 to 1979. It was led by Pol Pot and the Khmer Rouge.
Devaraja	A title, which literally means "god-king," that was given to the ruling members of the royal family in the ancient Khmer Empire. The kings were worshiped as gods by their subjects.
Junk	A flat-bottomed sailing ship used in China and throughout the Far East for both river and ocean travel and trade.
Khmer Rouge	The name, which literally means "red Khmer," that was given by King Sihanouk to communist activists among the Khmer people.
Krama	The black-and-white checkered cloth traditionally worn as a headdress by the Khmer people, particularly in rural areas. The Khmer Rouge favor red-and-white kramas.

Lamthon	The traditional national dance of the Khmer. It features slow, graceful movements of the hands and arms and involves almost no movement of the feet.
Monsoon	A strong seasonal wind that brings torrential rains to Cambodia from April to October and relatively dry weather during the rest of the year.
People's Republic of Kampuchea (PRK)	The communist regime that governed much of Cambodia, with Vietnamese backing, from 1979 to the early 1990s.
Phnom	Khmer for "hill."
Sampan	A small flat-bottomed river or harbor boat driven by one or two poles that are shoved against the bank or bottom. Sampans are used as houses and floating small businesses by families throughout the Far East.
Sampot	The traditional garment of Khmer men and women, which consists of a knee-length, wraparound skirt or sarong.
Trung trei	A fish farm located on a lake. Captive fish are fattened for sale in pens under the fisherman's home.
Wat	Khmer for "temple."

◄INDEX►